Rocket Science

by Richard Cohen

HOUGHTON MIFFLIN HARCOURT

PHOTOGRAPHY CREDITS: COVER (bg) ©Science Source/Photo Researchers/ Getty Images; 3 (b) ©Science Source/Photo Researchers/Getty Images; 4 (b) ©Enoch Seeman/Bridgeman Art Library/Getty Images; 5 (r) ©NASA; 7 (b) ©Kevin Wheal/Alamy Images; 9 (b) ©NASA; 11 (b) ©NASA; 13 (b) ©Science Source/Photo Researchers/Getty Images

Printed in Mexico

ISBN: 978-0-544-07328-9

2 3 4 5 6 7 8 9 10 0908 21 20 19 18 17 16 15 14 13

4500456330   A B C D E F G

Contents

Vocabulary	Stretch Vocabulary	
force	propulsion	drag
gravity	Newton's third law	escape velocity
	action–reaction principle	propellant
	thrust	combustion
	friction	ion

Introduction

Have you ever heard the expression, "It's not rocket science?" People use this expression to mean, "It's not very difficult." Obviously, many people think rocket science is such a hard subject to understand that other subjects are easy by comparison. It's true that it takes a lot of education to design and build rockets. But the basics of rocket science are not as hard to understand as you might think.

Until the 1960s, rockets seemed very new. Therefore, most people hadn't studied them. Today, rockets have become familiar, so it's easy to learn about them.

The fact is that rockets aren't even new. They're actually hundreds of years old! Let's find out how rockets work.

On July 24, 1950, the United States began launching rockets at Cape Canaveral in Florida.

Rockets Defined

A rocket is a vehicle that is powered by rocket propulsion. The basic principle of rocket propulsion is that a blast of high-energy material shoots out of the back end of a vehicle. This produces a force in the opposite direction, pushing the rocket forward.

Rocket propulsion relies on an important scientific law called Newton's third law of motion. Sir Isaac Newton, a British scientist, developed this law. It says that, for every action, there is an equal and opposite reaction. This is called the action–reaction principle.

Imagine that you blow up a balloon and pinch it closed with your fingers. You open your fingers and release the balloon. When you let go of the balloon, the air inside it shoots out in one direction. This is the action. At the same time, the balloon shoots in the other direction. This is the reaction. This kind of propulsion can work in outer space, too.

Sir Isaac Newton (1642–1727)

Using Force to Overcome Force

Force can be any kind of push or pull. Force that pushes a rocket upward is called thrust. Another powerful force, gravity, opposes the thrust and pulls the rocket toward Earth. The larger and heavier a rocket is, the greater the gravitational pull toward Earth.

Another force that opposes thrust is friction. Any time two objects rub against each other, they exert friction. A rocket moving through the air rubs against air molecules, causing friction. This frictional force that pushes against a vehicle is called drag.

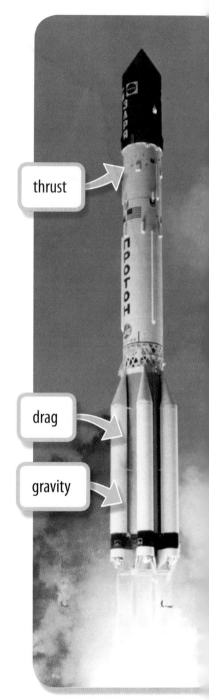

thrust

drag

gravity

Leaving Earth

In order for a rocket to fly into space, it must first overcome the gravitational pull of Earth. In daily life, nothing fully overcomes that gravitational pull—not even the highest-flying airplanes. That's because nothing travels fast enough. To overcome the pull of Earth, it is necessary to break free of gravity. How? Through velocity, which is defined as speed in a particular direction. The velocity necessary to break free of gravity is called escape velocity. Escape velocity on Earth is 11.2 kilometers per second (km/s), or just a little over 25,000 miles per hour (mph). Compare that to the speed of a big jet airliner, which is about 0.22 km/s (500 mph). A rocket needs to fly 50 times faster than a big jet!

Once the rocket has used escape velocity to enter into orbit around Earth, it no longer needs thrust.

Escape velocity varies with gravitational pull.

Escape Velocities	
Earth	11.2 km/s (25,038 mph)
Moon	2.4 km/s (5,321 mph)
Jupiter	59.5 km/s (133,018 mph)
Sun	618 km/s (1,381,600 mph)

Propelling a Rocket

In order to achieve escape velocity, a rocket needs a huge amount of thrust. Rocket propellant is the material that the rocket burns in order to make the force of thrust. Most rocket propellant is made of a mixture of chemicals that react together and produce combustion, or burning.

When combustion occurs, it gives off a sudden burst of hot gases that shoot out from the rocket. This causes the rocket to thrust upward. The thrust lasts until all the propellant is burned.

One of the most frequently used propellants is a mixture of liquid hydrogen and liquid oxygen. Hydrogen and `oxygen are gases at normal temperatures, but at extremely low temperatures they become liquids. Oxygen becomes a liquid at −184 °C (−300 °F). Hydrogen doesn't become a liquid until the temperature drops to −253 °C (−423 °F).

Liquid oxygen and liquid hydrogen require great care to keep them cold when stored.

Rocket Fuel

Why does rocket propellant need to be liquid rather than gas? The answer is simple: to save space. The atoms of an element are much closer together in liquid form than in gas form. Therefore, a cubic meter of liquid hydrogen contains much more burnable material than a cubic meter of hydrogen gas. Rockets need huge amounts of propellant, so rocket designers try to reduce the weight and volume of the rocket.

The rocket that took American astronauts to the moon had a thrust greater than the power of a line of train locomotives 322 kilometers (km), or 200 miles (mi). To gain that much thrust, the rocket burned an incredible 13,608 kilograms (kg), or 30,000 pounds (lb), of propellant per second!

Solid fuels were used in early rockets. However, solid fuel is much harder to control. Once lit, it keeps burning until it is completely used up. Solid fuel is best for rockets that need a single, big burst of power and don't need changes of speed or direction, such as model rockets.

Liquid fuels are easier to control. Rocket pumps, which send the fuel from the storage tanks to the engine, can pump a small or large amount of liquid fuel. This allows the rocket to change speeds and to burn the fuel over a longer period of time.

Going in Stages

The need to limit a rocket's weight is what makes rocket design tricky. Rockets today use lightweight materials strengthened by ribs. However, if a rocket is too light, it simply isn't as safe as a heavier rocket.

One solution is to build a rocket with stages. A rocket with stages is really several rockets stacked on top of each other. Three-stage rockets are the most common type of rocket. Each stage has its own fuel supply. When the fuel for one stage runs out, that stage drops off.

The first stage, which often uses solid fuel, provides energy for liftoff. After the first stage drops off, the second stage, powered by liquid fuel, takes over. The third stage takes the rocket into orbit or toward a destination. The rocket becomes much lighter at each stage, and less fuel is needed for acceleration.

Stages solve the problem of weight, because parts of the rocket drop off when they are no longer needed.

The Beginning of Rockets

The idea of staged rockets sounds modern, but it really isn't. The staged rocket was invented in 1555 by an engineer named Conrad Haas. In fact, the whole idea of rocketry is ancient. The first rocket may have flown in the 4th century BCE. The Greek scientist Archytas (428–347 BCE) supposedly built a bird-shaped device propelled by steam.

In the 13th century AD, Chinese scientists invented "fire arrows," tubes filled with gunpowder and attached to arrows. These arrows used the principle of thrust, so they can be called rockets. These early rockets first took flight in a battle against Mongol invaders. A Chinese legend says that a man named Wan Hu built a chair with 47 gunpowder rockets attached. He attempted to launch himself into space!

In India, in 1780, the Indian army successfully shot rockets toward the invading British army at the Battle of Guntur. In return, a British colonel, William Congreve, designed new rockets, including a kind that could be fired from ships. The British used these "Congreve rockets" against the United States in the War of 1812. Congreve rockets are even mentioned in the U.S. national anthem: "And the rockets' red glare . . ."

The Modernization of Rockets

In the 1800s and early 1900s, rockets became well-known to the public through science fiction stories by such writers as Jules Verne and H.G. Wells. Science fiction even inspired some young people to become rocket designers.

In 1903, the same year the Wright brothers flew the first airplane, Russian schoolteacher Konstantin Tsiolkovsky wrote a book about using liquid-propelled rockets to explore space. Then, an American, Robert H. Goddard, built the world's first liquid-propelled rocket. On its first flight on March 16, 1926, it flew for 2.5 seconds and rose 12.5 meters into the air. Goddard went on to design control systems for rockets and parachute systems to recover rockets that fell to Earth.

During World War II, Germany developed the V-2 rocket, which could carry a bomb weighing almost 750 kg (1,654 lb) for a range of 360 km (224 mi).

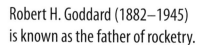

Robert H. Goddard (1882–1945) is known as the father of rocketry.

The Era of Space Flight

After World War II, the United States invited German rocket scientists to work for the Army. The leader of the V-2 team, Wernher von Braun, became the leader of the American space effort.

However, the Soviet Union was the first nation to launch a satellite into orbit. This was the Sputnik I, which launched on October 4, 1957. The United States then launched a satellite named Explorer I on January 31, 1958. Soon afterward, on July 29, 1958, the United States established the National Aeronautics and Space Administration (NASA).

The United States and the Soviet Union engaged in a furious "space race." The Soviets put the first human into space on April 12, 1961, when Yuri Gagarin flew one orbit around the Earth. The first American astronaut, Alan Shepard, took a 15-minute flight on May 5 of that same year.

On July 20, 1969, Neil Armstrong of the Apollo 11 mission became the first man to walk on the moon. Several Apollo flights took other astronauts to the moon. Then NASA decided to build a space shuttle. The first space shuttle launched in 1981. During the shuttle era, astronauts lived for long periods in space stations, conducting experiments and making repairs on satellites. NASA retired the shuttle design in 2011.

The Future of Space Flight

Since the moon landings, the United States and other nations have sent unmanned missions to Mars, Venus, and Jupiter. In August, 2012, the Mars rover Curiosity began transmitting amazing pictures of the Martian surface.

A promising advance in rocketry is ion propulsion. An ion is an electrically charged atom or molecule. Solar panels on the outside of a rocket generate electricity, which charges the atoms of liquid propellant. Then, magnetism pushes the ions out of the ship, creating a low level of thrust that can guide a spacecraft for thousands of days.

NASA's Dawn mission is using ion propulsion. Dawn is traveling to our solar system's two largest asteroids, Vesta and Ceres. The trip began in 2007. One day, more advanced types of ion propulsion may guide missions beyond the solar system.

NASA and other nations' space agencies strive to excel in the field of rocket design.

Test a Balloon Rocket

Gather the following supplies: a long balloon, a clothespin, tape, straw, string, pennies, and paper clips. Inflate the balloon and close it with a clothespin. Tape the end of the balloon to a straw. Attach one end of a long string to a solid support, such as a doorknob. Run the string through the straw. Attach the free end of the string to another support. When you release the clothespin, the balloon "rocket" will run along the string.

Test what happens when the rocket carries different weights or when it travels at different angles. What forces does the experiment demonstrate?

Write a Journal Entry

Imagine yourself as a rocket pioneer from any of the times or places discussed in this book. Write a journal entry describing a dramatic event you have experienced, such as your first launch. Include details about your invention, and describe what you look forward to in the future of rocketry.

Glossary

action–reaction principle [AK•shuhn ree•AK•shuhn prihn•sih•puhl] Every action creates an equal and opposite reaction.

combustion [kuhm•BUS•chuhn] Burning.

drag [DRAG] A force that pushes on a rocket in the opposite direction from the rocket's motion.

escape velocity [es•KAYP vuh•LAHS•uh•tee] The velocity that is needed in order for a rocket to break free of Earth's gravitational pull.

force [FAWRS] A push or pull that may cause a change in an object's motion.

friction [FRIK•shuhn] A force that acts between two touching objects and that opposes motion.

gravity [GRAV•ih•tee] The force of attraction between objects, such as the attraction between Earth and objects on it.

ion [EYE•ahn] An electrically charged atom or molecule.

Newton's third law [NOO•tuhnz THERD LAW]
The scientific law of motion, discovered by Isaac Newton, which states the action–reaction principle.

propellant [pruh•PEL•uhnt] A substance, such as fuel, that propels an object.

propulsion [pruh•PUL•shuhn] A means of pushing an object forward.

thrust [THRUST] A force that moves something forward.